Narcissism

Essential Information On Narcissists: Their Exploitative Tactics Like Gas lighting For Dominance And Control

(Recovery From Narcissistic Behaviors)

Normand Carter

TABLE OF CONTENT

What Is Narcissism?.. 1

Comprehending Individuals With Narcissistic Traits And Narcissistic Dispositions 14

Do Not Regard Individuals With Narcissistic Tendencies As Suffering From An Illness. 24

How To Improve And Rediscover Your Authentic Self...42

Narcissistic Abuse Recovery 49

What Is The Definition Of A Personality Disorder?73

The Experiences That Await You 84

The Pitfalls Of Interdependence And Achieving Liberation...100

Phases Of Rehabilitation Following Victimization By A Narcissistic Individual 120

Navigating Narcissistic Relationships.......................128

Type-Casting The Darkness..142

Strategies For Managing Interactions With Narcissistic Individuals. 160

What Is Narcissism?

Narcissism is often misconstrued as an excessive manifestation of self-assuredness, accompanied by an inflated self-perception and a heightened sense of significance. Nevertheless, beneath this outward facade lies an individual with a noticeably delicate sense of self-worth and a heightened susceptibility to critique. Although individuals with narcissistic traits may exhibit a deficiency in empathy and possess an intrinsic desire for admiration to achieve fulfillment, their primary objective is to seek approval. Set aside any entrenched biases you may possess towards narcissism, and immerse yourself in the tangible reality and concealed workings of individuals afflicted by this condition.

Narcissism can give rise to challenges in multiple aspects of an individual's life, encompassing but not limited to their professional endeavors, interpersonal connections, educational pursuits, and even their financial standing. Individuals afflicted with this disorder tend to experience a sense of disapproval and letdown when they are not bestowed with the admiration or preferential treatment that they perceive as rightfully belonging to them. Narcissistic individuals generally experience a profound sense of solitude due to their lack of empathy, leading to a tendency for friends, family members, and colleagues to distance themselves from such individuals.

Nonetheless, remedies are available for individuals afflicted with this condition. Regrettably, a considerable number of individuals with narcissistic tendencies remain undiagnosed due to their limited awareness and comprehension of their symptoms. Moreover, individuals' social circles including friends and family perceive this behavior not as a handicap.

Now, let us examine the indicators exhibited by individuals afflicted with this personality disorder, thus facilitating a more comprehensive comprehension on your part.

Symptoms

Kindly note that for an individual to be categorized as having narcissistic tendencies, it is necessary for them or the individual you are endeavoring to assist to exhibit at least five of the subsequent symptoms in order to meet the criteria.

This condition is among the various disorders present. It entails a state in which an individual possesses attributes that precipitate socially distressing behaviors and emotions which impede their ability to effectively engage in academic pursuits or establish and maintain interpersonal connections.

Individuals exhibiting traits of narcissistic personality disorder may present as individuals who possess an inclination towards ostentation, self-importance, and affectation. Frequently, you will find yourself engaged in one-sided conversations where others are unable to participate verbally. You are likely to hold a condescending attitude towards those in your vicinity, openly demeaning them. You may even regard everyone with an air of superiority.

Individuals diagnosed with narcissistic personality disorder often exhibit a sense of entitlement, believing that they deserve to have their desires fulfilled. Consequently, when their expectations are not met, they frequently respond with anger or impatience. Narcissistic individuals will assert that they possess the utmost in all aspects, such as the finest automobile, top-tier healthcare, the most exceptional residence, and so forth.

Nevertheless, simultaneously, a narcissist will encounter difficulty in managing critique, or anything they may interpret as critique. Narcissists will covertly experience sensations of vulnerability, disgrace, uncertainty, and humiliation. In their endeavor to attain relief, individuals may exhibit adverse responses, including contempt, anger, or the act of diminishing others. Certain individuals with narcissistic traits may experience periods of melancholy and despondency due to a sense of falling short of their self-perceived ideal standards.

The Diagnostic and Statistical Manual of Mental Disorders, commonly referred to as the DSM-5, is extensively utilized for the purpose of diagnosing narcissism by a significant number of practitioners. The following symptoms are outlined below.

A common characteristic encountered is an inflated perception of one's own significance. For instance, an individual exhibiting narcissistic tendencies may distort their abilities and accomplishments with the intent of garnering recognition as superior to others, despite lacking commensurate achievements.

Preoccupied with self-indulgent fantasies. Individuals with narcissistic tendencies often engage in elaborate fantasies featuring themselves as possessing immense power, exceptional intelligence, unparalleled physical beauty, an ideal romantic partner, or experiencing limitless achievements.

Narcissistic individuals may hold the belief that they possess distinct qualities or abilities that set them apart from others. Moreover, they may maintain that their true essence can only be comprehended by individuals or institutions of elevated status or exceptional nature. They readily display a condescending attitude towards others.

Individuals with narcissistic traits actively seek excessive admiration due to an inherent lack of self-worth residing within them. They hold the belief that their sense of value is derived from the opinions of others.

An individual exhibiting narcissistic personality disorder will possess a profound sense of entitlement. They hold the belief that they ought to consistently receive preferential treatment, expecting conformity to their dictates from others. They hold the conviction of their infallibility and perceive others as existing solely to fulfill their needs.

The previously stated symptom of entitlement is connected to the following one. Narcissistic individuals demonstrate a profound inclination towards exploiting others, willing to leverage anyone necessary to accomplish their objectives. They are willing to engage in opportunistic behavior to secure a job promotion, acquire a desired item like a watch or purse from a store, or exploit the generosity of a friend to attain their desires.

One characteristic that is often regarded as central to the profile of a narcissist is their profound absence of empathy towards others, or at the very least, their apparent absence of empathy. Despite the potential presence of this emotion, narcissists tend to actively suppress and disregard their own emotional experiences. They demonstrate a lack of willingness to acknowledge the sentiments and emotions of others, as well as the requirements of others.

Narcissists may hold the belief that others covet what they possess, or they may themselves become envious of others. A narcissistic individual will consistently refuse to accept anything less than first place and will never exhibit grace in the face of defeat.

Another definitive indication of a narcissistic individual is someone who displays a demeanor or disposition characterized by haughtiness and arrogance. Once more, this serves as an indication that they hold themselves in higher regard than others, or at the very least, it is commonly perceived in this manner.

This disorder is generally diagnosed during adulthood because narcissistic personality disorders necessitate a persistent pattern of behaviors and characteristics that extend beyond a duration of one year. A personality disorder is something that is long-standing and has an enduring pattern of behavior. The diagnosis of this disorder presents challenges due to the ongoing cognitive and physiological development in children and adolescents, as their brains undergo dynamic changes and maturation.

It is noteworthy that the occurrence of narcissistic personality tends to be more common among men, a fact that may come as a surprise to many. This personality disorder is believed to manifest in over 6.2% of individuals in the general populace.

Similar to many personality disorders, narcissistic personality disorder tends to diminish in severity as individuals age, with the most severe symptoms largely subsiding by the time the patient reaches their forties or fifties.

Although certain indications and characteristics of this disorder might appear to resemble mere self-assurance, it is essential to acknowledge that self-assurance and narcissism differ significantly. Confidence entails engaging in tasks that may present challenges, whereas narcissism manifests as elevating oneself above others and displaying disdain towards them. It entails prioritizing others over oneself.

Having acquired knowledge about the disorder, when would it be most appropriate to schedule an appointment with a medical professional?

Narcissistic individuals often fail to acknowledge the indications of their disorder during periods of elevated mood and contentment. They will persist in disregarding their symptoms due to a perception of infallibility and superiority over others. They will solely pursue medical intervention and guidance from a qualified practitioner upon experiencing symptoms of depression associated with their perceived rejections or criticisms.

Therefore, if you happen to identify with any of the aforementioned symptoms or find yourself experiencing depression or an profound sense of sadness, it is imperative that you proactively seek assistance from a dependable mental health expert.

Meanwhile, let us examine several factors that contribute to the development of narcissism and the anticipated outcomes when attending a medical appointment.

Comprehending Individuals With Narcissistic Traits And Narcissistic Dispositions

Consider narcissism as an exaggerated perception of one's own significance. It may prove challenging for one to perceive the behavior, due to its close correlation with confidence. It is commonly instilled in us that harboring self-love is highly beneficial. Therefore, what potential issue could arise in this regard? The distinction lies in the fact that while one of them constitutes an unhealthy conduct, the other one does not. An individual with narcissistic tendencies will hold an excessively inflated self-image and demonstrate a lack of regard for others; it is important to note that self-assurance does not necessitate a superiority complex. Receiving validation and recognition is what sustains a narcissist's emotional wellbeing. Lack of acknowledgement leads to the emergence of insecurity, which consequently manifests in varied forms of aggression. There are no limits to this overt demonstration of self-admiration. Numerous individuals with narcissistic traits exhibit a propensity to prioritize their unrelenting craving for attention over personal relationships, familial ties, and prospects in the professional realm.

The creature does not rest beneath the bed. The creature has the ability to rest in close proximity to your person.

Photograph credit: Sarah Richter

Strategies for Restraining Conduct

The parents' role is paramount in facilitating the child's understanding of moral distinctions. In the event that signs of narcissistic behavior arise, one can undertake uncomplicated measures to redirect the emotional aptitude onto the correct trajectory. To commence, it is advisable for a parent to explicitly address any occurrences of self-centeredness through verbalizing. This will bring attention to the action that requires modification. While it is essential to avoid any form of humiliation towards the child, the initial step towards acquiring a sense of limits is raising awareness. Subsequently, alternative remedies can be proposed.

Recognizing and commending a child's actions demonstrating generosity will serve to enhance and promote the recurrence of such behavior. Ensure that the child is cognizant of their virtuous behavior and is aware of the positive impact it has when exhibiting such qualities. Establishing a state of equilibrium between actions to avoid and actions to aspire to is essential in fostering mental clarity in a child. An excess of any singular element will invariably lead to an inherent lack of equilibrium.

Utilize effective methods to promote positive self-worth in children. Promote the development of your child's self-esteem and instill a strong sense of self-worth. Ensuring that a child comprehends that their self-value is not inherently contingent upon external validation or praise will serve as a proactive measure to mitigate instances of disruptive behavior. Having the understanding that these two matters are not intended to be intrinsically linked can prevent a child from developing a belief that he or she lacks value or worth.

Set a positive example! Young individuals have an exceptional ability to perceive and learn from their surroundings. If a parent exhibits narcissistic traits, it can be readily observed and internalized by the child. As a mature individual, it is crucial to exercise mindfulness regarding one's own behavior. The credibility of the argument diminishes when one fails to exemplify the principles they impart to their child. Having a shared understanding will prove to be advantageous, not just in the upbringing of your child, but also for your own personal growth.

Draw Attention to Narcissism

While actively nurturing your child, you may feel inclined to guard them from any harmful influences that may come your way. The desire to shield one's child from any form of negativity can often arise as an inherent instinct. Regrettably, this strategy is not feasible nor efficacious for circumventing narcissism. Rather, facilitate the child in observing the behavior. Provide an analysis of the reasons for its incorrectness as well as suggestions for alternative approaches. This represents a significant aspect of maturing and acquiring the essential abilities required for adulthood.

When deemed suitable, elucidate the notion of manipulation to your child as well. Through the adoption of this methodology, your child will cultivate essential analytical skills, enabling them to discern the distinction between ethical and unethical choices. Adopting such a mindset can help individuals avoid developing narcissistic inclinations. Establishing this trajectory at an early stage can greatly enhance the likelihood of future success for your child. He/she shall not be susceptible to exploitation or prone to developing such behaviors.

Acquiring knowledge about this particular behavior actually serves as a means of safeguarding oneself. Illuminating the nature of danger is a formidable task without prior familiarity with the danger. Acquiring awareness equates to obtaining knowledge, which in turn will enable your child to establish measures of protection. An egocentric child will perceive a need to demonstrate specific behaviors in order to validate oneself. By instilling in a child from an early age the notion that this is superfluous, you are bestowing tranquility.

Facilitating the presence of other individuals who share similar values in your child's early years will prove to be highly advantageous. Observing that individuals apart from a parental figure uphold the same conduct will impart a sense of reassurance. It serves as a means to substantiate your arguments and to immerse your child in real-life demonstrations of constructive conduct. These exemplary individuals can include relatives, acquaintances, and even mentors or educators.

There exists a specific social stigma associated with mental health and the choice to seek assistance, particularly when addressing issues concerning children. If you deem it appropriate to pursue the assistance of a professional, there is no inherent stigma in doing so. Narcissistic personality disorder (NPD) is a significantly severe psychiatric condition characterized by a notable degree of treatment refractoriness. Detecting it at an early stage and promptly seeking assistance will yield significantly greater results than permitting the child to develop with those same principles. Conventional talk therapy sessions have the potential to significantly benefit children. There are also sessions available which incorporate art as a means of further articulating emotions.

Receiving assistance at a young age is a considerably more logical choice than leaving the child to grapple with these emotions in solitude. This does not imply any shortcomings as a parent; rather, it indicates the degree of diligence and solicitude. Narcissism is a behavior that possesses the potential for amelioration if detected at its early stages.

Initiate a dialogue with the physician taking care of your child. You will have access to the most superior resources available in that location. The pediatrician should possess access to a selection of recommended therapists who are well-suited to your child's specific age group. Please bear in mind that therapy is a customary approach and there is no reason to experience any sense of shame or embarrassment. Notwithstanding the perceptions of observers, granting your child the opportunity to articulate these profound emotions is a constructive undertaking.

When it comes to children and therapy, the methodology will adopt a less rigorously clinical stance. Typically, the child is afforded the opportunity to engage in play with toys and engage in artistic endeavors such as drawing. There may be occasions where you will be required to be present in the room with your child throughout the session. Therapeutic interventions provide the child with a medium through which they may potentially channel and express their emotions in a more unrestrained manner. The objective is to provide support in implementing the constructive methods that the parent is already employing.

Do Not Regard Individuals With Narcissistic Tendencies As Suffering From An Illness.

In order to grasp the experiences of individuals afflicted with Narcissistic personality disorder, it is imperative that we ascertain the precise characteristics and traits of the individuals under discussion. Narcissism can be classified as a psychological disorder. Individuals suffering from this disorder exhibit a notable absence of empathy towards others, and in the event of provocation, their responses may not be amicable. Narcissistic individuals constantly seek attention and harbor the belief that they are paramount in their significance. Indeed, the Narcissist is incapable of grasping the significance of causing emotional distress to another individual. They lack the capacity for empathy, and a portion of their population is unable to comprehend the infliction of harm upon others. Individuals who suffer from this disorder can bring about a multitude of difficulties across all facets of existence. In various domains such as professional environments, educational institutions, familial settings, and interpersonal connections, individuals with narcissistic tendencies exhibit a belief that their personal needs take precedence over those of others. In the event that they do not receive the attention and admiration they believe they are entitled to, the situation has the potential to turn unpleasant.

The reality is that each individual possesses a certain degree of narcissistic tendencies, which serve as a catalyst for our self-care. However, should one possess an excessive preoccupation with oneself, it would result in seclusion from others and a sole focus on personal gratification.

Occasionally, discerning between an individual who exhibits self-centered tendencies and someone diagnosed with Narcissistic Personality Disorder can prove to be a challenging task. There exist numerous resources and compilations detailing the methods for identifying individuals with narcissistic tendencies. There exist individuals, including both professional psychologists and those with personal encounters with Narcissists, who have extensively documented various attributes employed in the determination of Narcissism. All individuals concur on several fundamental means of acknowledgment: The Narcissist is bound to be an individual who occupies the central position in the universe, wholly engrossed in their own being. In the event that you are engaged with an individual displaying extreme narcissistic tendencies, it is likely that they will perceive you as an object to be exploited, rather than recognizing your inherent humanity and the need for compassion and affection. Please bear in mind that such behavior is predominantly not borne out of malicious intent; instead, it stems from the fact that to a narcissistic individual, fulfilling their own needs is their utmost priority.

Therefore, in the event that Narcissists perceive that you possess the capacity to provide them with the desired level of attention, you will discover yourself captivated by their charms until they attain their intended goal. As they lack comprehension of conventional human interactions, once their objectives are fulfilled, they will cease to exhibit thoughtful behavior. The predominant etiological factor contributing to this disorder is childhood trauma or the occurrence of other significant and enduring life events. Despite typically possessing strong social skills, they face challenges in forming attachments. They can be encountered within various contexts, and exhibit remarkable adaptability in attaining their objectives. Narcissistic individuals possess the ability to adapt their identity in accordance with the circumstances. They possess amicable tendencies and easily establish harmonious relationships with others. Sometimes they can scare and intimidate, or they can even act like they really care about other people's well-being. They have the ability to entertain and liven up social gatherings; they possess a friendly and accessible demeanor. However, the actual situation contradicts this claim. Should you initiate inquiries about their personal life, they will invariably employ various tactics to evade such inquiries. If you attempt to approach, they will intercept your proximity. They do not possess the inclination to engage in lengthy discussions about their personal matters, and in the event of persistence, they will ultimately ostracize you.

Narcissistic individuals demonstrate a proclivity towards exerting control over others, all while skillfully portraying an appearance of caring and fostering amicable behavior. Their predicament does not arise from a dearth in social aptitude; rather, it stems from a deficiency in displaying empathetic attributes. A portion of individuals possess a desire for authority or the attainment of achievement, while an alternate group derives satisfaction from being esteemed. Nevertheless, should you fail to meet their expectations or prove insufficiently valuable, they will simply disengage. There are numerous factors that contribute to the difficulty of addressing Narcissism, particularly when one becomes aware that they are merely utilized as a mere tool to achieve a desired outcome.

In the case of individuals with Narcissistic tendencies, exploiting others is not merely a desire, but rather an inherent necessity. And they are indifferent to the potential reactions of others. Due to their perception of self-importance and elevated status, they believe that others harbor feelings of envy towards them, only to realize that they themselves are envious of others in the midst of such presumptions.

Narcissists frequently exhibit tendencies of excessive self-importance and a condescending attitude towards others. If one dedicates time to observing their conduct, they will discern that individuals with this particular disposition possess an alternative perception of confidence. Furthermore, unabashed self-adulation of such magnitude can remarkably influence others across various domains.

When does Narcissus cease to be a myth and instead become a child?

It is highly probable that during your time in academia, you would have inevitably encountered the widely known mythological tale of Narcissus. This disorder was given its appellation based on the aforementioned myth. Ovid, the poet, is attributed with the authorship of the Roman adaptation of this particular myth. To expound upon the psychological condition known as Narcissism, it is imperative that we thoroughly examine Ovid's narrative:

Narcissus was born of a river deity and a nymph known as Liriope. She sought insight into the prospective destiny that lies ahead for her son, compelling her to consult with a prophetic individual. She was informed that should Narcissus fail to acknowledge his own reflection, he would be endowed with an extended lifespan. Narcissus matured into an aesthetically pleasing individual and garnered affection from others. However, he believed that there was not a single individual to whom he would reciprocate such fondness. The gentleman possessed such captivating beauty that it even prompted the nymph Echo to develop feelings of affection towards him. Echo was afflicted by a curse that rendered her incapable of vocal communication. Her abilities were limited to mere mimicry of the sounds and words spoken by other individuals. As she pursued Narcissus through the woods, she endeavored to establish contact with him, yet she could merely echo his words. When the nymph materialized and endeavored to grasp Narcissus, her advances were rebuffed. The deities were filled with anger towards Narcissus, and thus sentenced him to experience rejection from all those he held dear to his heart. One day, during a hunting expedition, Narcissus stooped down to quench his thirst from a spring within the forest. He developed a deep affection for his own reflection as it appeared in the water. He was utterly astounded by the individual he encountered. He attempted to seize hold of the reflection, yet his efforts were ultimately in vain. Narcissus remained submerged in the water for an extended period of time. He was neither sleeping nor eating. He developed such a profound fixation on the individual he encountered that he initiated conversation with their reflection, vowing steadfast commitment without ever parting ways. As Narcissus was bidding adieu to his own reflection, Echo emerged and faithfully echoed his words. He passed away, and upon witnessing the nymph's sorrow, a blossom emerged at the site of his demise.

Numerous psychological studies employ this myth as a point of reference, and its various components possess significant symbolic significance. The tale of Narcissus garnered greater attention and utilization among scholars specializing in the field of human behavior, compared to other myths. For these individuals, the aforementioned myth symbolizes a range of contrasting concepts, including the juxtaposition of illusion and reality, the coexistence of passion and coldness, the paradox of desiring love while simultaneously rejecting it, the embodiment of both being a subject and an object of desire, and so on. Narcissus embodies a metaphorical reflection of self-awareness as a cessation of existence while illuminating the significance of empathy in one's personal growth. Furthermore, it denotes the paradoxical nature of self-indulgence and the dangers associated with an overemphasis on external attractiveness. Narcissus has been widely associated with the notion of detrimental self-admiration. Based on the findings of several researchers, it can be established that the Narcissus and Echo relationship served as the foundation for the Narcissistic family paradigm. In the narrative at hand, it is evident that both protagonists exhibit a lack of attentiveness towards the perceptions, auditory stimuli, and responsiveness pertaining to the well-being of one another. According to certain empirical studies, Narcissus can be interpreted as symbolizing the parent system fulfilling its own desires. There are several factors that can contribute to this occurrence, namely alcoholism, substance abuse, occupational stress, and mental health disorders, among others. However, in contrast, Echo symbolizes the younger generation. This child demonstrates unwavering determination in seeking the attention and affirmation of their parents, ultimately leading them to be perceived as an extension of their parents. In contrast to children residing in well-functioning households, children whose parents suffer from Narcissistic Disorder are compelled to fulfill their parents' expectations. These parents uphold the belief that it is incumbent upon their children to fulfill their desires, rather than the inverse. As they serve as exemplars for a child, they wield considerable sway over the child's perception and development. The presence of a role model is instrumental in facilitating a child's understanding of distinguishing between acceptable and unacceptable behavior.

On the other hand, children originating from families characterized by Narcissistic traits tend to develop into individuals who exhibit both reactive and reflective qualities in adulthood. The repercussion of children acquiring the understanding early in life that they must fulfill parental expectations is often the inhibition of their ability to place trust in their own emotions. Their emotions give rise to unease as they are unable to obtain any validation for their sentiments. It is customary to admire and emulate certain qualities of one's parents within reasonable limits. Nevertheless, within the dynamics of the Narcissistic family, this mirror symbolizes the child's inability to fulfill the parental expectations, consequently inducing a pervasive sense of inadequacy.

Individuals who have been brought up in families characterized by narcissistic tendencies often encounter challenges in establishing close and deep connections with others. They fail to cultivate trust during their formative years, leading to difficulties in establishing meaningful connections in their adult lives. Are you familiar with Maslow's hierarchy of needs? It constitutes a psychological framework devised by Maslow, a preeminent figure in the field of psychology. His framework delineates that the requirement for psychological and physical security is a fundamental aspect of fostering trust. When it comes to a child brought up in a household characterized by Narcissistic traits, ensuring their safety often entails the need to disavow trust, as opposed to the absence of learning to trust.

There exists a range of behaviors, such as the humiliation of the child and the consumption of alcohol to excess, which have the potential to elicit a detrimental situation for the child. This type of circumstance gives rise to impairments for the child, particularly when they are being brought up while the occurrence of this event becomes a routine.

Allow us to examine a tangible illustration. Presented herein is the narrative of Mary, an individual reared within the confines of a family characterized by Narcissistic tendencies. Mary remembers her mom. However, upon inquiry about her relationship with her mother, she responded, "my mother simply existed." Mary went on to elaborate that her mother carried out routine household tasks, yet she perceived their connection as distant and unattainable. Subsequently, Mary expressed a sensation of her mother's presence and concern, albeit to a limited extent. Mary came to the realization that her mother's response to significant life events seemed to be rehearsed and detached, as if following a preconceived notion of parental behavior rather than genuinely caring. Mary's narrative does not encompass the epitome of sensational maltreatment; instead, it serves as an exemplification of a parent who exhibits emotional unavailability. As Mary matured, it became increasingly evident to her that her mother demonstrated a lack of attentiveness towards her and an inability to meet her emotional requirements.

Still, there are many cases that illustrate abusive families. There exists a plethora of instances wherein overtly Narcissistic families are grappling with substance abuse pertaining to alcohol and drugs, as well as engaging in acts of incest and various other forms of assertive conduct.

How To Improve And Rediscover Your Authentic Self

One of the most noteworthy aspects of life lies in the fact that regardless of how entrenched one may become in an erroneous path, the opportunity to reverse course and embark upon the pursuit of one's aspirations remains ever-present. There is never a moment when one's age becomes a hindrance to envision new dreams and embrace an enriching existence. In the event that you find yourself on a path devoid of progress or purpose, do not hesitate to temporarily cease your journey and ascertain the optimal course to pursue. A new beginning in your life may take time, but it's all possible. Fortunately, we possess boundless capacity within our anatomies and intellects to channel our aspirations towards the attainment of our desired objectives. Adversity may occasionally undermine your self-worth and dampen your spirits, yet it can never diminish your inherent ability to rediscover your true identity: that of a cheerful, insightful, methodical, and intelligent individual, ready to be reawakened.

Each day, we navigate the varying currents of life as they sweep us along, encountering inevitable shifts and transformations. Occasionally, this alteration is unfavorable, propelling us towards an adverse outcome. However, on occasion, it is the alteration itself that acquaints us with substantial reservoirs of knowledge, imparting valuable lessons through firsthand encounters. During times of profound affliction, it is crucial to avoid becoming excessively preoccupied and succumbing to the notion that we are incapable of reclaiming our fundamental essence. This is particularly applicable if you perceive the passage of time and the depletion of your energy, leading to a potential inability to restore your former brilliance. You perceive that your prime years have elapsed and you are presently advancing in age, therefore it is more advantageous for you to persist on the unfavorable path, regardless of life's trajectory.

Fortunately, even individuals regarded as highly accomplished throughout history have been prone to making ill-advised choices that have steered them astray. They employed a visionary mindset, perceiving themselves as the victor and refraining from dwelling on the temporal, exertional, and energetic costs incurred due to erroneous decision-making. If one possesses a strong sense of discernment, one will come to the realization that individuals often experience a revitalization and begin to pursue their aspirations through methodical endeavours subsequent to their failures. Ultimately, it is widely acknowledged that these individuals attain greater success and garner global acclaim. Whether it is the paramount athlete, the most accomplished entrepreneur, or the wealthiest individual, these individuals have encountered hardships in their lives. Nevertheless, they refused to succumb to adversity, opting instead to meticulously regroup and forge ahead. An illustrative example would be the remarkable narrative of Steve Jobs, wherein he recounts significant errors and their consequential impact. He employed a Chief Executive Officer who subsequently terminated his employment due to disparate visions for Apple Inc., an enterprise established by the revered Steve Jobs. Nevertheless, Steve demonstrated unwavering perseverance in the face of adversity, refusing to succumb to the loss of his lifelong aspirations. In addition to his accomplishments, he achieved notable success through the establishment of renowned technology companies such as Pixar and NeXT.

This identical scenario is applicable to you in situations where you have endured a distressing existence with an individual exhibiting narcissistic traits. This individual, motivated by ill-intentions, exploited you for their personal gain. They showed indifference towards your aspirations. Indeed, their primary focus was on completely overpowering you and inflicting a lasting and profound impact on your existence. Instances of mistreatment result in diminished levels of self-assurance and diminished self-worth. It appears as though you are unlikely to successfully restore order to your life or attain contentment while also pursuing your personal goals, needs, and objectives. In its entirety, it appears to be a challenging endeavor to improve the state of your life. The underlying inference of this statement suggests that overcoming the effects of narcissistic abuse is no easy feat, as it necessitates transitioning from the lingering anguish of past experiences to acquiring the motivation required to propel oneself towards a more optimistic and promising future. The anguish that was inflicted upon you has not only shattered your spirit, but also undermined your identity, thereby placing you in a precarious predicament. It is perplexing how an individual whom one had regarded as a soul mate ultimately reveals themselves to be a cold-hearted oppressor, consequently giving rise to profound perplexity in the aftermath of the relationship. Like many victims, you may find yourself struggling to comprehend, questioning how these events unfolded under your watch. Alternatively, "Furthermore, how could they have subjected you to such actions while maintaining the façade of affection?" It is important for you to be aware that your bestowed qualities of forgiveness, compassion, and empathy have facilitated your ability to grant them the presumption of innocence. Now that you have become aware of the painful reality of abuse, it is crucial for you to strive towards genuine recovery and actively participate in the healing process.

Narcissistic Abuse Recovery

Get Away

One will encounter various challenging stages while being in a relationship with an individual exhibiting narcissistic tendencies. There may arise moments when one experiences profound feelings of mistreatment, degradation, and isolation, which may provoke a desire to surrender. You will experience feelings of extreme fatigue, diminished self-worth, and social exclusion. You shall experience profound anguish, yet concurrently demonstrate an aversion to confronting the harsh reality, thereby resorting to self-delusion in order to seek solace. However, over time, you will experience heightened dissatisfaction when you come to the realization that you had merely engaged in self-deception. There may arise instances in which one experiences a sense of confinement akin to being in a prison, with no perceivable means of liberation. This undertaking will indeed present difficulties, nevertheless, one must commence at some point. Commence by instructing yourself to develop resilience towards their self-centeredness. Presented below are a series of instructions to accomplish this task.

Exhibit resolute determination and embrace self-reliance, pursuing a life that aligns with your personal aspirations.

Do not permit discussions and arguments to deplete your emotional well-being and vitality.

Cease bestowing compliments, attention, and praise upon the individual, as these actions serve as the primary source of accolades for the narcissistic individual.

Limit the duration of your conversations with the individual. Narcissistic individuals derive pleasure from occupying the spotlight, and by actively interacting with them, you are inadvertently providing them with validation and sustenance.

Do not descend to the same moral plane as the narcissist. While I understand that they may be causing you considerable annoyance and you may be tempted to retaliate to teach them a lesson, I must caution against pursuing such an approach as it is not advisable. The narcissistic individual will derive pleasure from engaging in a reciprocal exchange with you, culminating in your eventual disadvantage. Please be reminded that the individual displaying narcissistic tendencies possesses a significant level of expertise in manipulating others, while you may not possess the same level of knowledge or experience in dealing with such behaviors.

Eventually, your presence may no longer suffice to meet the expectations of the narcissistic individual in your surroundings. They exhibit a proclivity to remain in one's vicinity solely when there is a favorable outcome to be obtained, and given that you are no longer serving as a source of gratification for their narcissistic tendencies due to their behavior and remarks failing to affect you, they will seek alternative sources elsewhere. As soon as they identify another individual, please be aware that your reputation will be unjustly tarnished. They will communicate to their future partner the negative aspects of their prior relationship and the mistreatment they endured, for the purpose of evoking sympathy from their subsequent partner.

After their departure, you will experience a phase of mourning during which you will begin to develop compassion for the individual displaying narcissistic traits. One will come to the realization that their behavior is a manifestation of their profound state of depression. There is no necessity to experience such emotions; every utterance or action of the narcissist is precisely calculated and meticulously planned. They do not act impulsively or out of a sense of hopelessness. They possess a precise understanding and intentionality in their actions. The narcissist's experience of depression typically arises once their resources are depleted, prompting them to actively seek out alternative forms of stimulation such as alcohol, drugs, interactions with the opposite sex, or indulgence in excessive shopping. Upon receiving their provision, they revert back to their usual state. Rather than indulging in self-pity, it is advisable to partake in the following activities to overcome the overwhelming sense of guilt that you are currently grappling with.

Maintain a healthy and active lifestyle while attending to the needs of your physical well-being.

Engage in a leisurely stroll and seek the company of individuals who will provide you with solace and wellbeing.

Engage in open and honest conversations with individuals whom you deem as trustworthy in order to alleviate your concerns.

We encourage you to express your emotions through tears and vocalizations for however long you may deem necessary.

Unwind by indulging in an extended bath or shower.

Attend a film screening or procure a movie through a rental service, as this will provide a diversion from the current happenings in your personal sphere.

Commence the practice of maintaining a journal—this will facilitate a deeper connection with your emotions and enable the release of those that do not serve your wellbeing.

Buy yourself something nice.

Engage in volunteer work, as it will expose you to the understanding that there exists a greater responsibility in tending to individuals who hold greater significance than your self-centered significant other.

Take part in alternative therapies such as Eye Movement Desensitization and Reprocessing (EMDR) or Emotional Freedom Technique (EFT). These therapies are efficacious in facilitating the release and resolution of distressing emotions.

Immerse yourself in the company of individuals who exude positivity, thereby instilling a sense of hope that there exists a promising future ahead.

Remove any belongings or items within your residence that evoke memories or associations with your partner.

In the event of your partner exerting control by dictating your wardrobe choices and permitting only the clothes of their preference, it is advisable to donate said clothing to charitable organizations and commence wearing garments that align with your personal taste.

It is now imperative that you redirect the focus and care which was formerly devoted to your narcissistic partner towards yourself.

Having recognized the presence of a narcissist, your subsequent course of action entails creating as much distance as feasibly attainable from their influence. This is the challenging aspect! As stipulated in the literature, individuals exhibiting extreme narcissistic tendencies lack any semblance of empathy. They exhibit a glaring lack of accountability for their actions, causing a pervasive sense of distress among those in close proximity to them within a short span of time. It appears highly improbable that they possess even a semblance of consciousness regarding their conduct, and it is further improbable that they will introspect deeply and resolve to modify their behavior.

Given your capacity for empathy and sincere concern for others, it is likely that you will be inclined to assist the narcissist in recognizing the futility of their behavior. However, it is imperative to recognize that this course of action is ill-advised. It will have adverse consequences for you, as it will prompt their defensive response and potentially persuade you into believing that you are the one at fault. It is highly improbable to attain equitable terms with an individual of profound narcissism, and retaining their presence in your life will perpetuate your unhappiness.

You are required to arrive at a decision promptly. Dissolving any bond can be a challenging endeavor, though it is relatively less burdensome to sever connections with romantic partners, colleagues, friends, and occasionally, even family members. Generally, you are not legally obligated to continue the companionship with these individuals in the majority of instances. For instance, instances where joint ownership of a property does not exist, shared business ownership is absent, no dependents are involved, or will administration is not underway. Once liberated from these circumstances, it becomes feasible to extricate oneself from such a relationship. Whilst it may prove to be a challenging decision due to one's genuine feelings towards the individual, it is imperative to recognize that remaining in a relationship that inflicts emotional harm is not befitting of any individual. Ceasing all communication entails the act of firmly shutting down all avenues of correspondence, encompassing physical and virtual portals such as windows, doors, and mailboxes. Implement a thorough social media block to prevent any communication on various platforms, while also exercising the discretion to disallow any form of contact via email, text, or chat. Should any omission occur, they will exert formidable efforts to regain your favor. Please refrain from perusing antiquated text messages or heeding voicemails. Listening to their desperate pleas and appeals may evoke a sense of sympathy within you, thus rendering you susceptible to the snare they have cunningly set. Once you sever your connection with them, every utterance they make towards you will stem from anger and manipulation, which hinders the process of healing.

While complete eradication of the memory may be unattainable, it is indeed a desire to relegate their presence to the recesses of one's cognitive faculties. Hence, it would be advisable to kindly request friends and family to refrain from discussing the individual in question or inquiring about any communication you may have had with them. It would be advisable to kindly request them to refrain from disclosing any personal information pertaining to yourself. The perilous aspect of individuals with narcissistic tendencies lies in their exceptional charm, which captivates the affections of everyone around them. It is highly probable that your acquaintances and relatives will struggle to comprehend the rationale behind your decision to terminate the relationship. Frequently, he will earn the favor of your acquaintances and relatives, utilizing this advantage to reestablish contact with you. He will appear at your parents' residence in a state of distress, expressing his confusion as to why you have inflicted this upon him. His plea will be to obtain her contact details merely for the purpose of initiating a conversation and comprehending his erroneous actions, with the intention of resolving them. In such circumstances, it will be essential for your dear ones to exhibit resolute determination and firmly convey that they shall refrain from disclosing any contact information.

During the initial phases of the separation, it is imperative that you refrain from excessive solitude. Initially, you may experience a sense of solitude. It is highly likely that you have been involved in a long-term relationship with this individual, and currently, you find yourself independently navigating life. Furthermore, excessive solitude is conducive to introspection, prompting one to question whether they have made suitable choices. Maintaining utmost focus and avoiding regression is of paramount importance during this period.

Do not squander valuable time by attributing blame to yourself and entertaining thoughts of alternative actions that might have altered the circumstances. Regrettably, this mode of thinking is not novel to your understanding. Individuals who have experienced abuse at the hands of a narcissist are often subjected to the belief that they bear sole responsibility for the circumstances they find themselves in. They dedicate significant amounts of time and effort towards discerning how they could enhance their performance or refrain from engaging in actions that may have contributed to this situation. Please be cognizant of the fact that altering the nature of a narcissistic individual is an unattainable feat, as it is beyond your jurisdiction to enact such a change. They have the ability to alter only their own being. The sole individual you possess the ability to alter is yourself, and it is to this aspect that your attention should be directed. Your thinking should be guided by the following steps: "You have previously been involved in a detrimental and unhealthy relationship; it has concluded and now it is imperative to prioritize your personal recovery."

Another sentiment that you will need to confront is the anguish of recognizing that your former partner did not genuinely harbor affection towards you. Love is inherently benevolent, devoid of any inclination to inflict suffering or anguish. This realization poses a formidable challenge to confront, leading to an internal sense of being unworthy of affection. You may begin to ponder whether you warranted such treatment. As difficult as it may be, dwelling on such thoughts proves to be futile and drains one's precious time and energy. One must carefully consider the objective evidence, irrespective of an individual's personal interpretation of love or their capacity to express affection. Based on your own set of standards, it is clear that you should never have endured such treatment. Finding genuine love with someone who has a personality disorder is an unattainable endeavor, as individuals with such disorders lack the capacity to experience love towards others, and even towards themselves.

When you find yourself contemplating whether your partner truly loved you, endeavor to shift your cognitive framework and commence affirming to yourself that you possess inherent worthiness of love, you hold intrinsic value, and there exist individuals who will wholeheartedly love you without seeking to exploit you on an intellectual and emotional level.

"Foster your Knowledge on the Subject of Mental Illness"

This book has merely skimmed the surface in its exploration of narcissistic personality disorder. Having a greater understanding of the condition will facilitate your ability to avoid finding yourself in a comparable relationship. Engage in extensive reading, conduct thorough online research, attend educational seminars, and explore various avenues in order to acquire comprehensive knowledge about this disorder.

Having two I's proves to be more advantageous than having just one.

To possess a narcissistic disposition does not imply an insensitivity towards others, but rather reflects a conscious decision to prioritize self-care and self-acceptance. Is that detrimental to your well-being? I am uncertain as I lack the expertise in this matter; my knowledge does not align with that of a medical professional. Does it have a deleterious impact on the individuals in your vicinity? Indeed, that could potentially be the case; however, if one were to consider it in greater depth, the same argument could conceivably be applied to fried foods and beverages with high caffeine content. In fact, everything except love is bad for you. If provided with a sufficient quantity of water, it is inevitable that you will succumb to drowning. When provided with an excessive amount of food, one tends to gain weight. If an excessive number of feline companions are acquired, one may find themselves residing in solitude indefinitely, occupied with knitting scarves and necessitating the use of a lint brush prior to every departure from their residence.

Fortunately, love is exempted from restrictions. The only outcome is a pleasant and euphoric sensation, and in the most extreme case, you may need to consume a Lipitor and rest in a chair briefly to alleviate any discomfort. Individuals often fail to fully grasp the immense influence that self-assurance holds. There exists a commonly overlooked and timeless belief: the supremacy of will over physical circumstances. It pertains to the notion of exerting dominion over all other facets within the universe. Have you ever tried to lift an object with your mind only to fail. It is likely attributed to a lack of sufficient belief on your part. I would appreciate it if you could locate a pencil. Please position it on a desk or a similar surface. Please proceed to shut your eyes and endeavor to shift everything, all the while maintaining a steadfast confidence in your ability to do so. Did it move? Certainly not; please refrain from making foolish assumptions. It is not within your capacity to manipulate objects using the power of thought. Nonetheless, due to your self-belief, your internal level of foolishness was slightly diminished. And that is the only thing that holds relevance, does it not?

When contemplating narcissism, it has been widely agreed upon by society that, similar to a high-quality bottle of wine or a cask of whiskey, it is preferable to keep it hidden in obscurity, only to be accessed during moments of festivity or following a burdensome day. This sentiment is commonly echoed by individuals who devote their time exclusively to home maintenance, referring to it as their "occupation." That's just wrong. It is widely acknowledged that suppressing emotions or keeping them concealed will inevitably result in their forceful release, akin to water rushing through a compromised dam. By adhering to that action, you shall be free from the burden of bearing the emotional baggage of others. Please be mindful that life can be likened to an airport where you are limited in the number of carry-ons allowed.

Please understand that I recognize the potential difficulty in accepting this information initially; nonetheless, it remains crucial to maintain a holistic viewpoint. There are individuals presently in the global community who do not possess a copy of this book. I require your assistance in procuring a copy for them. Therefore, to err on the side of caution, it would be advisable to purchase an additional copy.

It is widely believed that inspiration can be derived from a multitude of sources. The individuals in question reside on the western coast, don garments adorned with peace symbols, consume excessive quantities of alcohol and tobacco, and exhibit a propensity for falsehoods. Inspiration is not an ethereal force that hovers in the sky, awaiting to serendipitously land upon an individual; it does not possess the characteristics of a self-aware vehicle reminiscent of The Jetsons. It is imperative for individuals to actively seek and discover creativity on their own accord.

What Is The Definition Of A Personality Disorder?

In recent years, there has been intensified consciousness among professional therapists and counsellors regarding the prevalence of personality disorders. The prevalence of such occurrences remains uncertain. Nevertheless, it is rather disconcerting (excuse the wordplay) to observe an alarming proportion of individuals who appear to be afflicted by one or multiple personality disorders. The repercussions on their own well-being can be exceedingly detrimental, while the repercussions on their marital union or partnership can be nothing less than catastrophic.

Regrettably, there is a dearth of information pertaining to personality disorders, especially regarding their potential impact on marital relationships. A significant portion of the available information is exclusively familiar to certain professionals and practitioners specializing in marriage therapy. It is possible that a considerable number of individuals find themselves in a marital situation with a partner exhibiting symptoms of a personality disorder, all while remaining unaware of such a specific mental health condition. These individuals may lack knowledge regarding the symptoms associated with personality disorders, and consequently may be uncertain about the impact it may have on their own marriage, as well as how to address it appropriately. In this literature, my intention is to provide readers with a profound understanding of personality disorders, along with effective strategies for progressing in marital relationships and life holistically, particularly if one's circumstances are impacted by such disorders. Please be advised, though it must be emphasized that finding a feasible solution for your situation will undoubtedly pose a considerable challenge.

What precisely constitutes a 'personality disorder'?

The term "personality disorder" has been characterized as a phrase associated with psychobabble. It is a term commonly utilized by mental health practitioners, derived from the DSM-IV, which is a comprehensive guide known as the Diagnostic and Statistical Manual for Mental Disorders.

In this particular context, the term "disorder" solely pertains to an individual's behavioral pattern encompassing their cognitive, emotional, and behavioral aspects, as long as it impedes their ability to lead a wholesome existence. For instance, if an individual experiences a mild form of depression, it would not be classified as a 'disorder' until the extent of their depressive symptoms significantly hampers their ability to engage in routine activities.

One method of exemplifying this concept is by contemplating anxiety.

Anxiety is a prevalent issue that afflicts many individuals. The majority of individuals experience anxiety at some point in their lives. However, a vast majority of individuals do not acquire an anxiety disorder. The classification of a disorder would only apply if the individual's anxiety severely impeded their ability to lead a well-organized and functional daily life. Hence, a disorder can be defined as the disruption caused by a particular characteristic of one's personality, which exerts a detrimental impact on an individual's life, reaching the extent of significantly impeding their own existence as well as that of those in their vicinity.

An alternative manner of characterizing a disorder is as an aberration or deviation in cognition or conduct. For instance, when examining an individual struggling with depression, considerable adverse consequences can be observed in various aspects of their life and their capacity to perform as a conventional member of society. It is likely that they will exhibit a significant emotional reserve. They will encounter challenges in maintaining mental clarity and executing basic decision-making processes. They will encounter difficulty in maintaining focus and will be unable to engage in extended conversations with individuals. They may additionally discover that they require ample solitude and prefer spending a significant amount of time in isolation due to the arduousness of social interactions or being in a stimulating setting.

In the case of mild depression, individuals often exhibit a capability to function adequately and maintain a relatively conventional lifestyle. Nevertheless, an individual afflicted with severe depression will find it challenging to establish a proper sense of connection. At that juncture, it transcends into the domain of a disorder - when the individual's psychological and emotional well-being, alongside their conduct, adversely impacts their interpersonal connections, particularly with their significant other.

There are evidently alternative forms of personality disorder; however, anxiety and depression serve as conspicuous illustrations of the essence of a disorder. Similar consequences on interpersonal dynamics are observed in relation to other manifestations of personality disorders as well.

Sensitive beyond Imagination

This implies that even a minor offense towards them will have consequences. The lesson to be heeded is to never underestimate or overlook them.

Instead, it is important to render profound unease whenever one resorts to expressing criticism. Furthermore, ensure that your facts are thoroughly accurate. The individual displaying narcissistic tendencies exhibits an inadequate receptiveness towards any form of criticism. Nor will they ever. To these individuals, it is not regarded as a valuable opportunity for personal growth and development, but rather an intolerable transgression for anyone to bring attention to any shortcomings they may have.

They perceive themselves to be flawless and will maintain this perception indefinitely. If you choose to express criticism, it will be interpreted as an act of insubordination and a demonstration of inadequate understanding on your behalf. As a result, it will be necessary to administer appropriate sanctions without any ambiguity.

The manifestation of aggressive conduct often serves as the initial response for individuals with narcissistic tendencies once they perceive a deviation from their desired circumstances. This can manifest itself as a complete outburst of immediate verbal rage or, conversely, as the emergence of a withdrawn, sulky expression. Confronted with pointed gazes directed towards you, filled with an air of peril.

Furthermore, it is important to note that your presence will be significantly disregarded from that moment onwards, with the understanding that there will undoubtedly be subsequent anger in due course.

This constitutes an approach aimed at exerting influence over individuals by instilling fear, specifically the fear of being rejected.

An individual who possesses a strong sense of fear is highly inclined to comply with whatever is demanded of them.

This does not imply that you should refrain from criticizing these individuals;

rather, it suggests that you should overcome your apprehension towards their potential adverse response.

It will be less than pleasant, and it is prudent to be forewarned in order to avoid being caught off guard.

Do not anticipate them to demonstrate empathy or grasp the significance of your predicament or valid perspective. Engaging in such behavior is not a practice they typically partake in.

They hold the perspective that the average individual lacks the ability to exercise autonomy or possess substantial levels of discernment.

Particularly when those decisions are not prioritizing the interests of the Narcissistic individual. Therefore, they have to take control on your behalf. When there is a need for your perspective, they will readily offer it to you. There is no necessity for you to exert yourself in that specific endeavor either.

Subjecting individuals to unwarranted insults and humiliation is an experience that is universally undesirable.

Hence, when we embark on a lifestyle that entails persistently enduring such treatment from another individual solely to maintain their favor, it becomes a substantial predicament. It is imperative that nobody ever engages in this activity.

If their anger arises due to your refusal to assume responsibility for something that is not yours, allow them to express their anger freely. Their excessive anger is an issue that they must address and manage on their own.

This phenomenon is commonly known as assuming adult responsibilities. It does not fall within your purview, therefore refrain from attempting to rectify it. Given the duration of your tolerance towards someone's immature conduct, you might foresee a prolonged commitment ahead. The implication of this is that the elimination of any form of behavior necessitates a patient and enduring approach. It won't happen overnight. Additionally, there will arise numerous instances wherein you will ponder whether the endeavor is truly worth the exertion and hardship.

This inquiry can solely be addressed by you. Ultimately, the outcome hinges upon the extent of your aspiration to be treated with equity and basic human decency by that particular individual. Furthermore, the significance of cultivating a harmonious relationship with this individual cannot be overstated.

The Experiences That Await You

In the event that you have ascertained that you have fallen prey to the manipulative tactics of a narcissistic individual, and you are resolved to liberate yourself from their grasp, it will be imperative for you to gain insight into the challenges that will ensue as you embark upon the journey of healing. It is undeniable that you will experience a range of emotional distress, and it is these distressing experiences that I would like to address. By exploring them, my intention is to assure you that proceeding with this stage is not futile as you continue to recover.

These experiences are typical emotions, indicative of progress and an eventual improvement. Nevertheless, it is important to consider that the sequence of emotions mentioned may not necessarily unfold in a prescribed manner. Nonetheless, it is inevitable that you will encounter each of the emotions categorized herein.

1. Anxiety. A narcissistic individual inherently desires to be the one initiating the termination of a relationship. They seek to be the person who rejects or persuades you not to leave, as narcissists are averse to being denied. Nonetheless, regardless of the circumstances, concluding the relationship will unquestionably cause anguish and distress. The source of concern arises when there is uncertainty regarding his potential return and commitment to continuing the relationship. With the passage of time, he has become an integral presence in your life, and the abruptness of his departure may potentially inundate you. However, it is advised not to indulge in that. Have faith in your abilities to perceive that it has concluded, and indeed, it has concluded. Prepare yourself to communicate should he or she happen to reach out to you. It is

imperative to remember the importance of being resolute and upholding personal boundaries, as doing so will effectively help in mitigating anxiety.

2. Obsession. It is likely that as you disengage from that relationship, you may experience difficulty in maintaining focus. Within your mind, numerous inquiries reside, for which you presently lack adequate solutions. One may inquire whether he genuinely harbored affection for you. Was he cognizant of the impact his actions had on me? Is it possible that his intentions were rooted in affection, despite the harm caused? Could it be argued that I am not only mistaken, but that I am so far from being correct that it is not even feasible to consider my view as a possibility? Is there a means by which I could have contributed towards preventing the deterioration of the relationship? Which aspects of the relationship demonstrate authenticity? How is it possible that he has transitioned to a new stage of his life

with such rapidity? There are numerous inquiries.

There is a propensity for individuals to feel inclined towards revisiting and thoroughly analyzing past events, including contemplating alternative approaches to ensure the viability of the relationship. Therefore, you will commence the process of devising strategies, contemplating the notion that implementing alternative courses of action would have yielded more favorable outcomes. These phenomena are merely manifestations of fixation and do not accurately depict the true circumstances at hand. It is a transitional phase, and with the passage of time, you will navigate through it and emerge victorious.

3. Grief. This surpasses mere fixation or preoccupation, reaching an even more unsettling magnitude. Given the probable experience of profound despair that is likely to persistently inundate you whenever you attempt to contemplate

the deeply interconnected relationship you once shared with said person - whether it be your former romantic partner or a dear companion And one cannot refrain from longing for his presence. Furthermore, it is essential to acknowledge that the relationship you shared with him epitomized genuine romance, surpassing any previous experience by both you and your family members. Indeed, there is a possibility that you may come to believe that such an experience may never be replicated.

The intensity may escalate to the extent that you find yourself questioning your previous judgments and instincts. So, in most cases, your grieving comes in twofolds. Initially, it is necessary to experience a period of sorrow and acceptance surrounding the departure of your former partner and the subsequent dissolution of the relationship. The second form of grief pertains to consistently reflecting upon and contemplating ways in which you could have approached the relationship more effectively. This, conversely, implies a lack of genuine comprehension regarding the dynamics of the relationship's demise. It may be accurately stated that during that particular phase, your perceptions are compromised, causing a significant divergence from objective reality.

4. Loneliness. I am confident that you had anticipated this outcome even prior to discontinuing your efforts. The manner in which the abuse manifests itself is challenging to articulate, and comprehending the events can prove to be a formidable task. Despite the necessity of seeking advice, it appears that they lack an understanding of your emotions and thought process. Furthermore, in the event that an individual approaches you in an attempt to comprehend your current situation, it is highly likely that they will be unable to fully grasp it.

This lack of comprehension leads to your seclusion and instills a sense of requiring solitary moments. Believing oneself to be isolated in their experiences, without the presence of anyone to confide in, may lead to a inclination to avoid participation in various social engagements that could have otherwise contributed to one's personal growth and recovery. Your current state of impaired judgment will inevitably prevent the realization of such a possibility. Consequently, you will continue to place emphasis on your own self-development, the preservation of the relationship, and the wellbeing of your former partner. Engaging in this action will exacerbate your sorrow and amplify your negative emotions, leading to detrimental effects rather than benefits.

5. Doubt. Individuals in the process of recovering from the influence of a narcissist will commonly experience a significant degree of uncertainty. For instance, consider whether there has ever been an occasion where he acknowledged his wrongdoing and

subsequently made efforts to realign his attitude. How often? Perhaps you can consider a couple of instances. How about other periods? Regrettably, one's cognitive faculties do not tend to dwell on such temporal divisions; rather, the mind is preoccupied with fortuitous displays of benevolence. You will never recollect those instances when unfounded accusations were cast upon you, despite clear evidence firmly establishing your innocence. Even during those periods, he attributed the emergence of the issue to your irate responses and displays of anger.

One will not recollect the experience of being subjected to name-calling and assault as a result of envy. Conversely, you will commence conjecturing. You appear to be magnifying a minor concern, assuming complete responsibility for the situation, and, perhaps most significantly, questioning whether your former partner exhibits narcissistic tendencies. Many individuals who experienced this period later admit that once it had elapsed, they were able to gain a more comprehensive understanding of the situation.

6. Shame. Towards the conclusion, as you strive for ultimate recuperation, you may commence contemplating why you would have endured the prolonged exploitation by another individual. He inflicted harm upon you on multiple instances; you were subject to manipulation and domination. You navigated a succession of uncertainties, experienced public embarrassment, yet maintained composure, and persisted until being enlightened on the true nature of narcissism. To compound the shame further, you pondered the potential validity of his claim. Perhaps everything he stated is indeed accurate - that you are truly devoid of value. All these thoughts make you feel ashamed of yourself. One begins to develop a perception of oneself as the possessor of such attributes and proceeds to engage in self-criticism, even for aspects beyond one's sphere of control. Public speaking

often evokes trepidation, as one cannot ascertain the veracity of the claims made about the benefits of being vocal. Although it may not always be true that you are right in every aspect of the relationship, it would be unfair to hold you solely responsible for the unfortunate circumstances that unfolded.

7. Anger. The amalgamation of feelings including shame, uncertainty, apprehension, and even melancholy will gradually diminish; subsequently, you start to recognize that you have been exploited and maneuvered. Then what happens next? Rage is likely to engulf you as you allow yourself to deeply experience the profound anger arising from the afflictions and prolonged tribulations that have befallen you. Now that they are becoming increasingly evident to you, it is no longer a mere illusion. Instead of feeling the need to retrace your steps and attempt to make things function, you now feel compelled to return and confront the Narcissist.

It gets so severe that you start to think that the relationship even suppresses some of the pains and anger you were denied when the relationship was on. It irks you. Additionally, you desire to confront the individual referred to as your former partner, yet regrettably, it remains unattainable.

At this juncture, denial does not warrant contemplation. This is indeed factual information. You may begin to perceive the wounds, the indicators of anguish that were aimed towards you, without your prior knowledge. It would be advisable to seek the counsel of trusted acquaintances, who can lend a listening ear and provide guidance on potential methods of restitution.

8. Relief. Indeed, that moment shall arrive. Ultimately, as you distance yourself from the Narcissist, the noxious emotions that embed themselves within you gradually dissipate. You have ceased attributing fault to yourself; instead, you

hold the Narcissist accountable. Subsequently, the sense of burden within your heart begins to dissipate. You have reached a point where your happiness in life is no longer contingent upon being in his presence. Consequently, the cardiac system initiates a process of clearing out. Subsequently, the world begins to regain clarity and coherence to your perception. You perceive the notion of reconciling with him as morally reprehensible and unjustified.

Subsequently, the procedure commences in a comprehensive manner; you persuade yourself that there is a considerable distance to be covered, nonetheless, an atypical event transpires, leading you to affirm your determination to overcome the challenge at hand, thereby committing firmly to pursuing that objective. With time, you may come to acknowledge that erasing the events from your memory is not necessary. Rather, you will develop the resolve to heal and establish the relationship as it currently stands – as an unfortunate circumstance for you. This induces a greater sense of relief within you, prompting you to lament not having been aware of this information sooner. You are eager to actively participate in any endeavor that will progressively uncover your authentic essence.

9. Focus On Yourself. Moreover, it becomes apparent that one must prioritize self-care and personal growth. One could initiate the process by exploring a fresh pastime or engaging in regular visits to a fitness establishment. Initially, the prospect of engaging with unfamiliar companions might appear intimidating and hesitant due to the depletion or exhaustion of your vitality caused by a Narcissistic individual. However, recognizing that you have extricated yourself from the situation will provide you with a sense of empowerment. You will experience a heightened inclination to establish connections with individuals who have

previously brought you joy and with whom you aspire to reciprocate happiness.

Subsequently, you will come to comprehend the extent to which you were marginalized and your emotional requirements remained unfulfilled, subsequently rendering you incapable of enduring a relationship of similar nature in the foreseeable future. While striving to prioritize your personal growth, you display a reluctance to engage in any type of relationship. Instead, your desire is to cultivate a mutually beneficial partnership that places importance on the needs and desires of both individuals, rather than being one-sided. You possess a deep conviction in your ability to attain that goal, recognizing that the granting of such privilege lies solely within the hands of patients. You are aware that further acquisition is necessary, thus commencing your quest.

10. You will be provided with an alternative individual. Following a

comprehensive series of lessons, which we will discuss in detail subsequently, you will undergo a process aimed at restoring your previous state and ultimately returning to this stage. However, once you do, you will experience a sense of satisfaction. You are now tasked with identifying the attributes that will facilitate the attainment of an appropriate companion, and recognize that a successful partnership primarily hinges on shared objectives and mutual comprehension, devoid of any derogatory language or instances of emotional or physical harm.

Engaging in this activity provides added enjoyment, and upon experiencing it, one would realize the immense satisfaction that comes with complete recuperation. Along with that stage comes a sense of ease and autonomy that is invaluable and irreplaceable. However, may I inquire as to whether you are interested in understanding the reasons behind the difficulties associated with severing ties with a narcissistic individual? You might have undoubtedly contemplated. Well, numerous individuals have pursued that same approach as well; nevertheless, it appears that no definitive response has been found, although there are indeed potential solutions. Those solutions will provide a clearer understanding of how to gracefully withdraw before circumstances diminish.

The Pitfalls Of Interdependence And Achieving Liberation

To begin with, could you kindly provide a definition for codependency? Undoubtedly, you have encountered this particular term on numerous occasions, presumably equating it to the concept of narcissism; however, could you provide a precise definition of its meaning? What is the purpose of including the 'co-' particle? To begin with, codependency denotes a reciprocal relationship. It is possible that the feeling being reciprocated may not be love itself, rather it is the meeting of a mutual need, a complementarity that has resulted in the perfect match.

What are the underlying factors that cause the codependent individual to be attracted to and become ensnared by the narcissistic individual? Individuals with these characteristics often experience diminished self-worth and perceive themselves as unlovable. Consequently, individuals can readily become ensnared in the narcissist's allure and manipulation, as these are the initial tactics employed by narcissists. The narcissist possesses an acute ability to detect signs of one's vulnerability and dependency, even from a considerable distance, and adeptly maneuvers this knowledge to their advantage. They present themselves as a compassionate individual and shower the less confident person with praise, fostering a deep admiration that will remain steadfast. The individual who exhibits codependency tendencies typically possesses a heightened sensitivity and a proclivity for prioritizing the gratification of others. They are inherently attracted to the magnetic charm of narcissists and may initially experience a sense of gratification upon perceiving the presence of a formidable protector. Certain individuals who exhibit codependent tendencies derive actual satisfaction from being accommodating and fulfilling the demands of a narcissistic individual, whereas others struggle with asserting themselves and establishing personal limits. This final aspect holds great significance within the context of this relationship. Both the narcissist and the codependent exhibit inadequate boundary establishment. On the other hand, despite the narcissist's excessively self-centered mindset, the codependent perceives themselves as lacking capability, competence, or worthiness, thus succumbing to manipulation due to their susceptibility. The individual characterized as codependent lacks a profound sense of personal identity. The narcissist possesses the capability to effortlessly manipulate individuals into perceiving themselves as unattractive, unintelligent, unskilled, incompetent, and so forth. The self-perception of the codependent individual is indistinct enough to incorporate notions such as truth.

Generally, individuals who exhibit codependency tend to possess limited capacity in effectively managing the emotional states and personal requirements of others. It is not difficult to elicit feelings of guilt from them, given their inclination towards caregiving that leads them to internalize the problems of others. One possible alternative formulation in a formal tone could be: "Possibly the most perilous aspect inherent in a codependent relationship resides in the intricate dynamics of projection and projective identification." While the narcissist engages in the act of projecting their insecurities and flaws onto others, the codependent not only internalizes these ideas as personal attributes, but also proceeds to exhibit behaviors that validate and reinforce the projection. As an example, the individual with narcissistic tendencies might exhibit the act of projecting fragility or unattractiveness. The codependent individual's physical appearance may or may not be aesthetically pleasing. Nevertheless, they often experience a sense of diminished strength and vulnerability, rendering them highly susceptible to genuinely internalizing such notions about their own capabilities. As the process of projective identification unfolds, individuals begin to exhibit behaviors that suggest a negative self-perception, such as doubting their attractiveness and having a distorted body image. The narcissist promptly affirms and reinforces this sentiment, simultaneously providing assurances to the codependent individual regarding their attention, particularly during the initial phases of the relationship.

Individuals who exhibit codependent tendencies typically originate from familial circumstances characterized by instances of abuse or the exertion of control. They are consequently ingrained with an unconscious inclination to pursue analogous patterns in interpersonal connections. The codependent individual experiences adversity as a result of being subjected to abusive behavior. Concurrently, they find solace in knowing that their counterpart seeks to exert dominance. It elicits a sense of enhanced security for them. Hence, when the narcissist displays controlling tendencies, the codependent unconsciously replicates familiar patterns, thereby remaining within the confines of their comfort zones. Assuming personal responsibility for their own lives would pose greater difficulty. Individuals who are codependent often exhibit challenges in effectively expressing their needs and commonly lack an established framework for establishing intimate connections. They acclimate to particular behaviors and subsequently exhibit automatic repetition of patterns. Due to their limited understanding of the concepts of love and appreciation, they are able to tolerate mistreatment.

The connections forged in the codependent state are predicated on necessity rather than on shared values and genuine compatibility. An individual of this nature experiences apprehension towards solitude and seeks companionship to alleviate it. They possess a deficient understanding of their own values. They act out of fear and insecurity more often than not. Individuals of such nature may also exhibit inclinations towards depression or obsession. Once they become ensnared, it is susceptible for them to experience a sense of vulnerability as they fixate on the subject of their fondness and may perceive that anything would suffice. In this scenario, the abusive behavior exhibited by the narcissist appears comparatively preferable to the unfortunate consequences of being forsaken or experiencing solitude. Codependent individuals, in the same manner, exhibit an estrangement from their own emotions as they are unable to genuinely discern their own values. Often they cannot even tell how badly hurt they feel by the narcissist's selfishness and mistreatment. They possess a heightened sensitivity to the emotions of others. Therefore, they possess a few maternal inclinations, and they exhibit a propensity to cater to the emotional and practical demands of the narcissist.

Typically, it is when the abuse escalates to severe manifestations and the codependent individual experiences heightened emotions, that they express their desire to liberate themselves. Intense suffering and previous experiences of distress can motivate individuals to actively pursue professional assistance or explore alternative means of safeguarding their well-being. What actions or strategies can an individual with codependent tendencies implement? What strategies can be employed to liberate oneself from the influence of a narcissistic individual, as well as mitigate one's own self-sabotaging inclinations?

The initial phase involves engaging in introspection and penetrating the various defensive barriers erected by the codependent individual. The individual in question must acknowledge that they were ensnared in a toxic relationship and confront their challenges with utmost sincerity. It requires considerable exertion and introspection to possess the ability to discern beyond various forms of rationalization, such as statements like 'Nobody is perfect.', 'Life is suffering.', 'Happiness is non-existent.', 'Everyone encounters difficulties in relationships', and so forth. It is imperative that individuals refrain from making broad generalizations, instead taking ownership of their own experiences and recognizing the potential and desirability of cultivating healthy relationships. The subsequent action that a codependent individual should undertake entails engaging in a sincere and introspective conversation with oneself, with the aim of comprehending their own emotions. Considerable emotional distress may manifest itself, however, it is crucial for the individual to gain awareness of the profound anguish experienced and the burdensome emotional baggage borne, originating from both the narcissistic influence and their personal history. Confronting distressing emotions is an essential aspect of the journey towards achieving inner healing. In order for the codependent individual to achieve a state of well-being, it is imperative that they engage in an examination and evaluation of their previous emotions, encounters, and ways of relating. It would be prudent for individuals to carefully scrutinize their familial surroundings, consider the manner in which their parents interacted with them or with each other, and evaluate any potential subconscious influences that may have shaped their adult relationships.

The subsequent phase entails reestablishing a connection with the individual's authentic needs and desires. Despite the presence of emotional masochism in codependents, once they attain an understanding of the detrimental effects it can produce, they possess the ability to liberate themselves from its grip. Thus, even in instances where one derives partial gratification from pain, the involvement in narcissistic connections inevitably undermines their self-esteem, leaving them devoid of any sense of self-value. Codependency typically entails consequences that extend beyond simply deriving pleasure from being mistreated or harmed by another individual. An individual of this nature is likely to exhibit substandard academic or professional achievement, a diminished social circle, a detrimental perception of oneself and outward projection, and a limited number of genuine companions. In addition to that, the absence of any prospects for the future, coupled with a profound sense of discontentment and a pervasive feeling of emptiness across various facets of their lives. Therefore, it is imperative for the codependent individual to gain a thorough understanding of the profound consequences resulting from their detrimental relationship patterns. Should you find yourself confronted with such a circumstance, it is prudent to reflect upon whether your desire truly lies in seeking distress and turmoil, or if your aspirations are better aligned with leading a gratifying and accomplished existence. Force yourself to choose. The narcissist potentially subjects you to a fluctuating range of intense emotions. Nevertheless, what are your genuine requirements? Wouldn't you desire to receive comprehensive training and secure a lucrative employment opportunity? Do you not desire to attain financial stability and derive pleasure from life's indulgences, all while avoiding the burden imposed by the narcissistic ego? The responses to these straightforward inquiries often become evident when the individual entangled in codependency has the opportunity to raise them and engage in a sincere self-reflection. What would be the consequence if one were to introspect and affirmatively acknowledge their genuine fondness for pain? In that case, you ought to consider procuring specialized services tailored specifically to fulfill your explicit desires, rather than allowing it to consume your entire existence.

The subsequent course of action entails the exploration of one's authentic values and priorities. What brings about happiness in your life? How would you define the appearance of your ideal self? What are your true priorities and desires? There exists a pronounced disparity between an individual's requirements and their principles. Typically, our ethical principles serve as the foundation of our character, bestowing upon us a steadfast sense of self that endures over the course of time as our distinctive brand. Reflect upon your true identity and the person you aspire to become. Do you sincerely desire to become a wreck? A weak person? An individual possessing diminished self-confidence and harboring skepticism regarding their own capabilities? Please document your desired occupation, should you have one. Should you encounter challenges in accessing your core values, a valuable alternative approach would be to inquire within yourself about the qualities you most adore in others. Doing so will allow you to unearth the aspects that hold utmost importance to you. Engaging in such a process of self-exploration can provide valuable insights into one's aspirations and desired identity. Acquire the ability to foster such attributes within yourself rather than solely appreciating them in others.

The subsequent course of action entails distancing oneself from detrimental surroundings and individuals displaying narcissistic behavior. This may prove to be a challenging situation, as it could potentially involve the difficult decision to separate from your abusive spouse. Nevertheless, it is a transformation that you have a responsibility towards. It is imperative that one safeguards their personal boundaries as psychological detachment alone is not truly attainable. It is necessary for you to physically relocate and establish a complete disconnection from the narcissist. It is imperative that you completely eliminate any avenues of communication, as the toxic psychic connection must be severed entirely in order for any form of healing to be attainable. Certainly, certain individuals may find it necessary to pursue diverse avenues of self-sufficiency, such as obtaining alternative employment with a higher salary to cover personal expenses or acquiring new skills through professional development opportunities offered in different geographical locations. Nonetheless, if you possess a genuine desire to liberate yourself, managing change becomes achievable. You will discover the resources to achieve self-sufficiency and thrive autonomously. It is advisable to refrain from swiftly transitioning between relationships, as doing so increases the likelihood of encountering comparable pitfalls and recurring patterns. Please exert maximum effort to take care of yourself, seek solace independently, and prioritize your healing above all else. Engage in new relationships only once you have overcome personal suffering and no longer experience feelings of threat. In order to foster a loving and healthy relationship with a new individual, it is imperative to possess a sufficient level of emotional security.

During the period in which you are not yet prepared to embark upon a new romantic commitment, it is advisable to seek the company of individuals who genuinely hold affection for you. Allocate quality time to be in the company of your family and friends, engaging in conversations centered around poignant encounters, until such time that you are able to release and overcome the emotional burdens associated with said experiences. In order to invigorate your life, consider embarking on novel and stimulating endeavors such as engaging in extensive travel, expanding your social circles through interpersonal encounters, immersing yourself in a diverse array of literary works, indulging in cinematic experiences, partaking in newfound hobbies, and exploring the artistic realms of galleries. The objective is not becoming ensnared in one's past trauma, but rather maturing and moving beyond it. The sole means by which this can occur is through your conscious investment in an array of captivating endeavors, which will necessitate greater effort from you and afford you significant cognitive enlightenment. Uncover your genuine interests - the opportunity exists regardless of the timing. Your true passion was certainly not the narcissist. Once you commence the process of fundamental self-reconstruction, you can consign that chapter of your life to the recesses of memory, resembling an unpleasant reverie.

Phases Of Rehabilitation Following Victimization By A Narcissistic Individual

Individuals who have been subjected to narcissistic abuse articulate their encounter with spending time in a relationship with a narcissist as an emotionally charged, highly volatile, and cruel expedition akin to riding a roller coaster. Once a victim successfully extricates themselves from the perpetrator's influence and the stronghold they held over their life, they anticipate the cessation of the harrowing encounter and its turbulent nature. Regrettably, the cessation of this situation is not immediate, and the affected individual discovers the fallacy in their belief that it has concluded.

The process of recovering from a relationship characterized by narcissistic abuse is a gradual journey that necessitates the passage of time and is marked by both favorable and unfavorable phases. To successfully extricate oneself from the toxic relationship, one must devote effort, time, and unwavering determination.

Sentiments towards the Former Partner

Irrespective of the entirety of your abuser's impact on your life, it is not within your capacity to instantly extinguish the deep emotions you harbor for them, in the manner of flicking off a light switch. This holds true in the case of a narcissistic former partner, due to the tactics of manipulation employed in order to evoke intense emotional reactions in the targeted individual.

Upon your departure from the relationship, you faced considerable hardships and demonstrated admirable bravery in making that choice. Nevertheless, the termination of the relationship did not diminish the affectionate emotions that you claim to still possess. Avoiding involvement in the relationship presents an equal challenge as it elicits feelings of disorientation, sorrow, and bereavement.

The conclusion of any relationship, regardless of its nature, resembles a demise and necessitates the grieving process. The relationship has terminated, and it requires a certain degree of acknowledgment in order to accept and comprehend this fact.

You will fight the longing to pick up the phone and reawaken the feelings and reignite the flame that was the reason you were drawn into the relationship in the beginning. You will experience the inclination to revisit and resolve matters, despite being fully cognizant of the unrealistic nature in which you have imagined the outcome to unfold.

The experience of longing to reconnect with one's former partner, all the while being subjected to the harsh treatment endured in the past, can be an agonizing ordeal. You are presently experiencing discord and experiencing a state of perplexity in a manner consistent with your previous situation in the relationship (A Conscious Rethink, 2019).

One's heart may perceive a lingering affection towards the individual who callously inflicted harm, while the intellect acknowledges that the abusive nature of their actions necessitates the acceptance of closure; their disregard for the consequences inflicted upon you becomes apparent. It is imperative that you maintain a substantial distance and refrain from returning under any circumstances.

This dialogue entails an individual who has experienced narcissistic abuse and is currently engaged in the process of recovering, engaging in introspective conversation. The prolonged and potentially insoluble nature of the reciprocal exchange of dialogue is worthy of consideration.

There exist divergent perspectives on the identical circumstance. One perspective emphasizes the positive aspects of the bond with your abuser, while the other perspective centers around the factual portrayal of the relationship and its ultimate outcome.

There are measures that can be taken to disrupt this oscillation of emotions and hasten the process of healing in order to resolve the impasse and achieve closure in relationships tainted by abuse. Below, I have provided a set of guidelines that you can adhere to:

Please document all of your convictions concerning the relationship that are obstructing your advancement.

Provided herein is an illustration depicting a compilation of individuals who have experienced adverse circumstances or harm:

I accept full responsibility for enduring such severe mistreatment.

I ought to have exerted more effort towards resolving the situation.

They are exhibiting superior treatment towards their newfound love when compared to me. It is likely due to the fact that person possesses superior qualities in comparison to my own.

I will not be able to encounter another individual who would render me a sense of uniqueness.

This compilation comprises the sentiments and emotions that a survivor will experience when severing ties with their perpetrator, rooted in their innermost sentiments. The victim harbors a desire to regain the positive aspects of their past relationship with their ex, as it existed during the period of harmony. This represents the affective aspect that experiences the discomfort that individuals are unwilling to confront or acknowledge.

The victim's relationship has concluded, leaving them with a sense of an irretrievable loss in finding another affectionate partnership, and the shattered prospects of an idyllic future with this individual. This is their perspective derived from the abuser's narrative regarding any involvement in additional relationships.

Navigating Narcissistic Relationships

There exist numerous justifications supporting the decision to remain in a relationship with a narcissistic partner. Some factors include offspring, extensive duration of commitment in the marital union, shared financial assets, involvement in business endeavors or multiple enterprises, feelings of uncertainty, and limited economic assistance following the dissolution of the marriage. Notwithstanding the underlying rationale behind your choice to remain committed to your partner, it is imperative to acquire the skills and discernment required to skillfully manage these relationships, thereby fostering your emotional and psychological welfare.

Having a narcissistic partner exhausts your happiness, tranquility, and vitality. It is arduous engaging in repeated efforts to gratify this individual without success, yielding negligible outcomes and limited alterations. Upon perceiving a sense of progress, one inadvertently regresses tenfold to the initial starting point. So, what strategies can one employ to maintain their mental well-being while remaining in a committed relationship with a partner who exhibits narcissistic traits?

Shift Expectations

The initial step that needs to be taken is to modify your expectations. Given your knowledge of their incapacity for emotional intimacy, it is imperative that you maintain a superficial level of engagement with them. Please adhere to discussing superficial subjects such as the meteorological conditions, objectives as a couple, forthcoming weekend plans, or allocated time for a romantic outing. Please be aware that they will not meet your emotional requirements for compassion, empathy, and comprehension. They lack the ability to navigate their emotional realm, thus rendering them unaware of where to initiate their actions. Consequently, it can be anticipated that they will acquire the ability to navigate your [whatever it refers to].

Your significant other might not grasp your preferred method of expressing love, nor will they value and encourage your aspirations. Indeed, should you choose to share with them your aspirations and future endeavors, it is highly probable that their response would be characterized by derisive and disparaging remarks, steeped in sarcasm and negativity. In a comprehensive manner, it must be understood that one should not anticipate the presence of an ideal confidant who embodies unwavering support, affection, esteem, keen perception, and nurturance toward one's aspirations, desires, and ideas.

May I inquire about your current occupation? How can one ensure the fulfillment of these needs while opting to remain in a relationship with a narcissistic partner? Adjust your expectations and anticipate that your needs will be fulfilled through nurturing relationships with friends or family. Seek the support and validation of the reliable social circles who value and acknowledge your aspirations and ideals. Develop a discerning understanding of whom to seek support from, and nurture those beneficial interpersonal connections in your existence. Devote your emotional resources to cultivating connections that inspire and motivate you to pursue your aspirations and objectives. They will serve as your pillars of support during moments of emotional distress within your romantic relationship or marital union.

When one alters their expectations and ceases to anticipate the satisfaction of those emotional attachments that they yearn for, an occurrence occurs. You have relinquished the compulsion to exert excessive control over various aspects within the relationship. You develop a reliance on your own capacities. You become enough. A voyage of self-compassion can be embarked upon, which is truly a magnificent endeavor to undergo, particularly in the midst of a disheartening dynamic where one's partner engenders feelings of being unlovable and lacking worth.

As your expectations undergo a shift, you will observe a gradual dissipation of your frustrations. You no longer demand. Hence, stress and, significantly, disappointment are no longer experienced by you. One experiences a sense of disillusionment as a prevalent emotion in the presence of a narcissist. Each time, your aspirations soar, only to be abruptly engulfed by an unforeseen tide of disillusionment.

As one becomes more acquainted with their partner's habitual narcissistic traits, they acquire the ability to discern the timing of potential confrontation and anticipate forthcoming disagreements. You will have the capability to identify instances where gaslighting and denial are employed. Being aware of what to anticipate can effectively mitigate the extent of disappointment experienced. By harboring fewer assumptions and expectations regarding your spouse or partner, you can effectively diminish the likelihood of experiencing disappointment.

Importance of Boundaries

Frequently, when we contemplate the concept of relationships, we envision a sanctuary or refuge. You desire a partner who embodies a sense of security, creating an oasis where you can seek refuge and freely divulge your emotions, assured of being met with empathetic and sincere attentiveness. However, this does not hold true in the presence of a narcissistic individual. They will use your moments of weakness and vulnerability as weapons against you. During those occasions, they will exploit such moments to degrade, diminish, and disgrace your humanity.

This situation ultimately presents only one option for you - the establishment of boundaries. What strategies can be employed to establish boundaries? Make yourself a priority. The self-centeredness of the narcissist necessitates avoiding enabling behaviors that prioritize their needs and wants. Rather, prioritize your own needs. Please prioritize the well-being of your mind and mental health. Please establish appointments for your therapy sessions, attend the gym, and engage in activities that bring you pleasure. Direct your attention towards the pursuits and pastimes that invigorate and bring you a sense of satisfaction. Ensure that these matters are given utmost importance and integrated into your daily and weekly schedule.

Another crucial aspect of establishing boundaries involves refraining from excessively dedicating oneself. A key factor contributing to your feelings of mental and emotional exhaustion is the tendency to continually expend your energy and resources, leading to a state of depletion. Rather than bestowing all of your energy onto others, I suggest allocating a portion of that affection and care towards oneself. Bestow your affection and provide sustenance for emotional well-being to those who reciprocate your love and value your presence.

Do not permit your partner to exploit you, even if you possess the capability to assist them. Do not make unnecessary efforts to accommodate your partner. Instead, wear emotional armour. Do exercise restraint in divulging excessive emotional sentiments. Maintain a straightforward and surface-level approach. Can one anticipate difficulties in implementing these provided responses and behaviors initially? Yes. It will prove to be a challenging endeavor, and you may succumb to temptation due to the emotional sway exerted by your lingering hopes, particularly when your partner exhibits signs of empathy.

You may find yourself inclined to veer towards your compassionate nature and extend empathy towards him, however, eventually this approach will prove to be counterproductive. Narcissistic individuals will habitually regress to their intrinsic tendencies of engaging in gaslighting, dehumanization, diminishment, shaming, derision, a lack of empathy, and denial, among various other behaviors. Please bear in mind that, on the whole, a narcissist's acts of kindness are typically motivated by a self-serving agenda. They exhibit inherent self-centeredness and consistently prioritize their personal interests.

Remain observant and work diligently to recognize your partner's narcissistic tendencies, enabling you to anticipate their behaviors. Furthermore, a key aspect encompasses the acquisition of skills related to effective responses. Please bear in mind that you should prioritize yourself in this particular relationship dynamic. It is imperative that you take heed of your own welfare and steadfastly strive to achieve your aspirations and objectives, irrespective of the opinions or perspectives your partner might express. Devote your life to yourself, directing your attention towards endeavors that bring you delight and fostering connections that foster your personal growth and prosperity.

If you opt to terminate the marriage or relationship, it would be prudent to exercise discernment in your approach. A divorce involving a narcissistic individual can escalate into a highly contentious, adversarial, and retaliatory process. The individual exhibiting narcissistic traits will actively seek to undermine your well-being, and in cases where children are involved, anticipate the likelihood of engaging in a legal dispute for custodial rights. I would like to offer you a single word of advice—make the necessary preparations. Ensure you are adequately prepared on emotional, intellectual, and financial fronts. Seek legal advice. Conduct your necessary research and investigation without disclosing it to your partner. Alternatively, failure to address this issue may result in their harboring resentment, thus significantly complicating the entire procedure. To rephrase the sentence in a more formal tone, you could say: "Alternatively, fortify yourself with emotional resilience and adequately prepare yourself."

The aforementioned information is of paramount importance for your acquaintance, as it is quite common for women to be romantically involved or married to individuals displaying narcissistic traits, often without comprehensively identifying such behaviors. You are in a state of despair and isolation, lacking understanding from others, which leads to a perception of inadequacy. You perceive a sense of psychological distress and are uncertain about the course of action to alleviate it or seek assistance from reliable sources. While perusing through this literary piece, you shall experience a profound sense of comprehension, wherein you shall ultimately be able to assign a label to actions that undermine your self-worth, identity, and emotional well-being.

Let us persist in excavating and performing the necessary tasks.

Type-Casting The Darkness

It is possible that you have encountered various individuals with narcissistic tendencies and observed their inclination towards self-centeredness and lack of empathy. Nonetheless, it is important to acknowledge that narcissists can exhibit different behaviors and traits. In order to effectively engage with these individuals, it is essential to familiarize oneself with the two distinguishable categories of narcissists - the grandiose and the vulnerable. While it is true that both categories of narcissists share some common characteristics, such as an inherent sense of entitlement, preoccupation with oneself, and a distinct lack of empathy towards others, they do exhibit noteworthy distinctions. Although a grandiose narcissist possesses an inflated self-perception, displays pretentiousness, exhibits an overt sense of superiority, demonstrates arrogance, exploits others for personal gain, and craves admiration, a vulnerable narcissist typically adopts a defensive stance, experiences insecurity, is prone to shame, hypersensitivity, anger, and hostility, endures feelings of loneliness, and possesses low self-esteem.

Therefore, can we conclude that one category surpasses the other in terms of quality, or is it more appropriate to assert that one category is more detrimental than the other? Given the pronounced nature of grandiosity and the concealed nature of vulnerability, the former appears to possess a greater level of commendability, at least superficially, when compared to the latter. Nevertheless, there is further substance to be considered. An individual with grandiose traits of narcissism exhibits an unwavering commitment to maintaining their identity and resists any compromise in accommodating others in various circumstances. If there exists any expectation or probability for change or enhancement, it primarily lies within the realm of the susceptible form of narcissism. Individuals who exhibit vulnerable characteristics may find it beneficial to seek professional therapy and counseling, as their inclination towards exerting dominance over others may not be as pronounced. Nevertheless, both categories of individuals pose a challenge in their interpersonal connections. Residing alongside a narcissistic individual is both undesirable and poses a threat to personal wellbeing. Hence, it is prudent to comprehend the subtleties of their attributes.

The Five Factors of Personality

Prior to delving into a comprehensive examination of grandiose and vulnerable narcissism, it would be prudent to examine the five-factor model (FFM), a framework that is applicable to a wide spectrum of individuals to varying extents. When an individual consistently manifests a particular persona, it engenders self-perceptions, traits, values, and exerts an impact on the expectations of their social milieu. The comprehensive five-factor model can additionally assist in forecasting an individual's reaction to individuals in a general sense, as well as challenges and high-pressure circumstances of various nature. The identification of the causes and resolution of narcissistic qualities and Narcissistic Personality Disorder

(NPD) relies upon the integration of various personality and trait theories.

- Extroversion (also known as extraversion)—is a personality trait characterized by a strong inclination towards sociability and high levels of energy. Individuals of this nature typically possess a high level of confidence, exude charm, and are articulate in articulating their thoughts.

- Neuroticism pertains to the experience of sadness and depression. Individuals exhibiting elevated levels of neuroticism demonstrate a propensity for experiencing heightened emotional distress, exhibiting increased levels of apprehension, and encountering difficulties when it comes to effectively managing various forms of stress.

- Agreeableness—characterizes an individual of a personality predisposition inclined towards agreement, cooperation, and altruistic behavior. An individual exhibiting a considerable degree of agreeableness tends to possess qualities such as empathy, compassion, and a constant willingness to accommodate the needs and desires of others.

- Openness—reflects inquisitiveness, attentiveness, and ingenuity. This individual possesses an inherent inclination to thoroughly examine novel avenues, experiment with unexplored endeavors, and exhibit a receptiveness towards embarking on adventures.

- Conscientiousness—characterizes an individual who demonstrates exemplary organization, discipline, attention to detail, and profound thoughtfulness. They always strive to avoid situations where they are ill-equipped or unprepared.

Currently, individuals who exhibit varying degrees of the aforementioned characteristics can be classified as narcissists, with the exception of "agreeableness," as the fundamental nature of narcissism inherently precludes agreement with others. A narcissist can be an extrovert, who likes to meet new people, and be opinionated and assertive. However, when these traits are accompanied by pride, selfishness, and insensitivity, we can think of a grandiose kind of narcissist. Conversely, an individual who is inclined towards introversion and values solitude may be referred to as a susceptible narcissist if they actively seek recognition for their unique qualities and exhibit a tendency to attribute their misfortunes to external sources.

A narcissist with grandiose tendencies is inclined to possess characteristics of extraversion, openness, and conscientiousness, whereas a narcissist who is vulnerable tends to exhibit greater neuroticism. A type of narcissism characterized by vulnerability is deficient in all other personality traits except for intellect. Individuals who exhibit grandiose narcissism tend to display traits that are deemed socially acceptable and positive, resulting in a comparatively elevated state of well-being and presumed stability. In contrast, vulnerable narcissism differs in its manifestation, characterized by social disfavor, maladaptive tendencies, and predominantly depressive symptoms. Although they exhibit starkly contrasting traits, both these personality types present challenges in cohabitation. These two types are not well-suited for interpersonal relationships due to their lack of sensitivity towards the needs of others.

To effectively cope with individuals exhibiting narcissistic personality traits, it is imperative for a survivor of abuse to acquire a profound comprehension of such individuals. By obtaining knowledge of the abuser's traits, the individual being victimized can mentally equip themselves for the potential behaviors and dynamics that lie ahead in their relationship. By means of foreknowledge, their cognition and physiology can prepare for the impending conflict. The victim shall not experience astonishment when encountering the undesirable conduct, but instead possess the capacity to confront it in a composed manner, devoid of anxiety, and furthermore ensure their own safety against any subsequent attacks.

Chapter Four

Three suggestions for effectively communicating when seeking to end a romantic relationship without undue difficulty.

In some manner or another, it is comparatively more straightforward to sever ties with an individual if they have committed some form of wrongdoing against you. Should your partner begin to undermine you, you are fully justified in your decision to end the relationship without the need to validate it.

However, life is not consistently uncomplicated. Occasionally, the manifestations of a relationship dissolving are more subtle and challenging to comprehend. Occasionally, there are instances where one is unaware of the precise reasons behind their decision to separate, yet they are certain that it is necessary.

There are several communication techniques that can aid you in determining the appropriate discourse when it becomes necessary to terminate a relationship.

1. Strive for Clarity and Brevity

It is widely acknowledged that the phrase "We need to talk" typically signifies an impending conversation of a negative or uncomfortable nature. Thus, I implore you to display resilience and refrain from evading the core matter at hand. Endeavor to refrain from prolonging the distress by meticulously enumerating each motive and subsequently concluding with the statement "..thus, I opine it would be prudent for us to terminate our relationship." Throughout the entirety of the explanation, you are engendering the false notion that you are still endeavoring to reconcile the situation. Initiate by establishing clarity, followed by delving into the underlying justifications, if necessary. To the best of your knowledge, they have arrived at a comparable conclusion - and a fundamental affirmation, "Indubitably, I concur with your observation," concludes the discourse. You can say:

I believe it is necessary for us to part ways.

I have been experiencing a profound sense of dissatisfaction in our relationship and I believe it would be prudent for us to contemplate taking a temporary hiatus."

2. Practice Transparency" "Embrace Candidness and Integrity" "Promote Openness and Truthfulness" "Foster a Culture of Honesty and Transparency" "Encourage Frankness and Sincerity

It is highly improbable that you would argue in favor of your partner deceiving you; therefore, it is advisable to exercise sound judgment and honesty when providing reasons for your decision to separate. In the context of communication, it is advisable to inform the concerned party of the exact point at which the disconnect occurred and to be candid in discussing the matter. If by any chance you have recently grown apart, it would be advisable to clearly and truthfully communicate to the individual where you believe your values and goals diverged, and the reasons explaining the lack of compatibility. Especially, if you happen to be uncertain about the reason, but still feel the need to separate, it is imperative to ascertain that as well. It is important to bear in mind that being candid does not serve as justification for being unkind. For instance, supposing that your associate is presently lacking in attractiveness to you, it is unnecessary to express, "I believe you are repulsive." Instead, you can provide a response that preserves your associate's dignity. You can attempt:

I no longer have the same positive sentiment towards you as I did initially.

3. Utilize Self-Reflecting Communication

Although it may be true that "I am the sole responsible party in this situation," this assertion often comes across as an evasion tactic. Regardless, it is advisable to make use of a multitude of "I" statements, as "you" statements can easily come across as accusatory. "You no longer demonstrate active listening." places responsibility on the other individual, whereas "It seems that I struggle to effectively communicate with you" acknowledges some personal accountability. This does not precisely equate to assigning blame - in fact, striving to determine a suitable approach for incriminating either oneself or the other party is typically futile and abhorrent.

When taking all factors into account, it may be necessary to examine how your own choices - as well as the actions of your partner - have contributed to the current state of affairs that necessitate a separation. Please bear in mind that at times, life circumstances may pose challenges that impede even the most amicable relationships. It is important to note that the conclusion of a relationship does not necessarily indicate its failure. People undergo ongoing phases of personal development throughout their lives, with no guarantee of consistent growth and alignment between individuals. You can say:

Lately, I have been experiencing a significant amount of uncertainty regarding our relationship."

I am no longer experiencing feelings of happiness and joy regarding our relationship, and I believe it is in our best interest to part ways.

The Main Thing

The manner in which you articulate your thoughts carries more weight than the actual content of your words. During the process of separating from someone, it is likely that both parties may experience a great deal of anguish, therefore it is advisable to make a sincere effort to convey your sentiments with utmost compassion. If you can exercise restraint in responding to your partner, you are significantly more likely to reach a mutual understanding of the reasons behind the need for separation. This will assist both of you in preserving and transforming your relationship into a cherished remembrance rather than a lasting emotional wound.

Strategies For Managing Interactions With Narcissistic Individuals.

The concept of narcissism lacks an appealing quality, hence, it is only natural to harbor a inclination to steer clear of individuals displaying narcissistic traits. Nevertheless, there will be numerous instances in one's life wherein they will inevitably encounter these individuals or even endure a considerable duration alongside them. Potential candidates for this role include your mother-in-law, your superior at work, or even your recently acquired roommate. Engaging in an interaction with a narcissist can have its redeeming qualities, provided one possesses the necessary skills to navigate such encounters.

For example, the leader characterized by narcissism demonstrates a propensity for excessive control. He possesses a great deal of charm and employs manipulative tactics, using counterfeit confidence to impress society. The self-centered leader possesses the capacity to engage in extensive networking endeavors and is inclined to do so in order to acquire the attention and admiration of a wide range of individuals. Narcissistic leaders have a propensity to exhibit anger and frustration in situations where they perceive a loss of control and influence, or when they are excluded from social engagements.

It is important to note that numerous prosperous organizations and businesses are led by individuals displaying narcissistic traits. It is not surprising, as they possess the charisma and self-assurance necessary to successfully execute it. Anticipate instances when their emotions may reach an extreme extent, occasionally in an unacceptable manner. Periodically, it will come to your attention that yourself and your fellow subordinates are tasked with undertaking the more arduous aspects of the workload.

To effectively manage the presence of the narcissist in your life, a recommended strategy is to employ flattery and praise as a means of appeasement. This strategy is highly effective when dealing with the narcissist, who is renowned for employing manipulation techniques. Should you believe yourself incapable of accomplishing the task at hand, recall the genuine underlying justification for pursuing it.

Exercise pragmatism when establishing expectations with an individual exhibiting narcissistic tendencies. Keep in mind that they are artful manipulators, so they are definitely going to try and weasel their way into turning things in their own favor. When dealing with the presence of a narcissist in either your professional or personal environment, it is imperative to establish explicit boundaries from the outset.

Permit the narcissist to fully absorb all the attention, particularly in instances where you desire their assistance. Narcissists have acquired a reputation for being lacking in competence, yet when exposed to public attention, they will go to great lengths to obtain approval. Please be aware that they have a preference for individual work rather than group collaboration. If it becomes necessary for them to contribute, you may consider mentioning that you will be sharing updates about the team's collective efforts online, allowing for a natural process of cooperation to take place.

Alternatively, it is advisable to refrain from posing threats to their sense of self-worth, as this could potentially trigger aggressive behavior. Several instances have been recorded wherein individuals who have openly criticized narcissists have become targets of their vindictive actions. Exercise extreme caution and discernment when delivering feedback to an individual with narcissistic tendencies. A suggestion I would propose is to adopt a tone that conveys a sense of levity and wit when offering feedback to an individual displaying narcissistic tendencies. Given that individuals exhibiting narcissistic traits employ humor as a means to garner attention and admiration, one can also utilize this strategy to effectively convey their message to them.

Is my significant other displaying narcissistic tendencies?
Taking all factors into consideration, it can be challenging to identify an individual exhibiting NPD, particularly when one has a close personal relationship with them, even if they possess knowledge regarding the officially prescribed diagnostic criteria. In order to assess the presence of NPD, a duly certified professional typically must

perform a standard psychiatric evaluation.

Nevertheless, possessing knowledge of the symptoms associated with NPD can assist you in gaining a broader understanding of your relationship. Presented herewith are a number of cautionary indicators to be vigilant of, along with recommendations regarding appropriate courses of action to be undertaken.

Initially, they were quite charming.

Individuals diagnosed with Narcissistic Personality Disorder (NPD) often display a propensity for exhibiting grandiosity and engaging in imaginative thinking. Initially, your relationship may have appeared reminiscent of a narrative from folklore. Possibly, they lavished you with flattering remarks or professed their affection for you during the initial month.

Despite the recent initiation of your romantic relationship, they may express admiration towards your intellect or underscore the significant harmonization between the two of you.

Nedra Glover Tawwab, LCSW, the director of Kaleidoscope Counseling in Charlotte, North Carolina, elucidates that narcissists hold the belief that only exceptional individuals possess the capacity to fully comprehend and value them.

Weiler advises exercising caution when encountering individuals who begin with excessive assertiveness. Indeed, we all derive pleasure from the sensation of being deeply desired. However, genuine love necessitates cultivation and maturation.

It is highly likely that you are correct in holding the belief that it is premature for them to possess genuine affection for you. Alternatively, according to Weiler's counsel, if you believe that individuals lack sufficient acquaintance with you to genuinely experience love, it is likely that their sentiments towards you are indeed lacking.

In the initial stages of a relationship, individuals exhibiting Narcissistic Personality Disorder (NPD) will make endeavors to establish fragile connections.

• They assert their dominance in the conversation by proudly highlighting their achievements.

Individuals diagnosed with Narcissistic Personality Disorder exhibit a magnified perception of their own significance.

As per the professional opinion of Jacklyn Krol, Licensed Clinical Social Worker at Mind Rejuvenation Therapy, it has been observed that individuals with narcissistic traits derive satisfaction from incessantly boasting about their own accomplishments and triumphs in a grandiose manner. This behavior stems from their deep-seated conviction of being intellectually superior to others, which further contributes to their display of self-assuredness.

As per the expert opinion of Dr. Angela Grace, an eminent clinical psychologist holding multiple advanced degrees including a PhD, MEd, BFA, and BEd, it has been observed that individuals with narcissistic tendencies often tend to embellish their abilities and magnify their achievements in these accounts, all in an attempt to garner admiration and praise from others.

Moreover, their excessive self-discussion impedes their ability to focus on your needs.

As per Grace's account, this caution comprises of two components. Your partner incessantly discusses themselves and neglects initiating a conversation regarding your experiences.

Consider these matters: When engaging in self-discourse, what transpires? Do they engage in subsequent interactions regarding inquiries and display a genuine inclination to gather further information about your background? Alternatively, are they centering the entire discussion around themselves?

www.ingramcontent.com/pod-product-compliance
Lightning Source LLC
Chambersburg PA
CBHW050232120526
44590CB00016B/2051